The Tongha... Railway

Peter A. Harding

The Railway Enthusiasts' Club special train "The Compass Rose" at Ash Green Station on October 5th 1957, with Drummond M7 class 0-4-4T No.30051 and pull-and-push set No.721. M.H.Walshaw

Published by

Peter A. Harding

"Mossgiel", Bagshot Road, Knaphill,
Woking, Surrey GU21 2SG.

ISBN 978 0 9523458 0 0
First published 1994. Reprinted with amendments 2019.
© Peter A. Harding 1994.
Printed by Binfield Print & Design Ltd.,
Binfield Road, Byfleet Village, Surrey KT14 7PN.

Contents

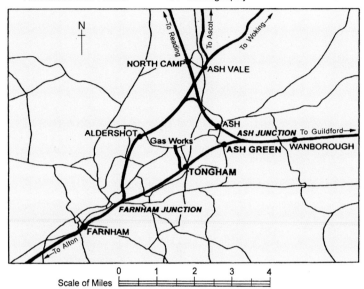

Scale of Miles

Bulleid Q1 class 0-6-0 No.33019 passing the former station at Ash Green en route for Tongham on December 24th 1960, a week before complete closure.   D.Lawrence

Introduction

The single track railway which ran from Ash Junction to Farnham Junction in Surrey and passed through pleasant countryside at Ash Green and Tongham (see map opposite), was originally part of a double track through railway from Guildford to Alton, first opened by the London & South Western Railway from Guildford to Farnham in 1849, and then to Alton in 1852. The railway was extended in 1865 from Alton to link with the main London to Southampton line, 2 miles north of Winchester.

When Aldershot was transformed in 1855 from a small remote heathland hamlet into a vast military camp, the stations, first at Ash Green, and later Tongham, were very much involved as a supply base for building materials.

In 1870, Aldershot received its own station on a new line opened from Pirbright Junction on the main London to Basingstoke line, to link with the original line between Tongham and Farnham, at what became known as Farnham Junction. Once this line opened and a spur added giving Ash direct access to Aldershot in 1879, services on the section between Ash Junction and Farnham Junction dwindled and, although a short branch was opened from Tongham to serve the Aldershot Gas Works in 1898, the line became an almost forgotten byway.

In 1930, the line was singled. With the electrification of other lines in the area, the passenger service to Tongham and Ash Green ceased in 1937. Although remaining open for goods, and also to serve the Gas Works, the section from Farnham Junction to Tongham was taken out of use in 1954 and the line finally closed in 1960.

I hope that this booklet will be a suitable reminder of this almost forgotten railway which, like many similar lines which experienced the same fate, are fast vanishing from our countryside.

Maunsell U class 2-6-0 No.31627 at Ash Junction with the Tongham - Guildford goods train on September 25th 1953.   S.C.Nash

3

History of the Line

During the early to mid 1800's, farmers in the area around Tongham, Farnham and Alton were extensively involved with growing hops, which had become the most important industry in the district. Beer was brewed locally and transported by cart to Winchfield Station on the main London & South Western Railway (LSWR) line between Basingstoke and Farnborough, then by train from Winchfield to London. With hop growing and other agriculture in mind, plus the possibility of carrying stone quarried at Alton, the LSWR applied to Parliament to build a branch line from their station at Guildford to a field at Alton (near the road to East and West Worldham) with intermediate stations at Ash Green, Tongham, Farnham and Bentley. The line was authorised on July 16th 1846, and the LSWR also planned to connect the new branch with their main London - Basingstoke route by building a line through Pirbright and joining up at Ash Green, but this section was never sanctioned.

The contractor appointed to build the Alton line was Thomas Brassey, a well known figure at the time, who was responsible for the construction of several other railways in the area, including the line from Guildford to Godalming. The consulting engineer was the LSWR's Joseph Locke, who had succeeded Francis Giles in 1837, while the resident engineer was a Mr.Vance, who was described as a bearded giant of a man with an intimidating character.

Meanwhile, the Reading, Guildford & Reigate Railway Company (RGRR), supported by the South Eastern Railway, opened their line from Reading to Farnborough on July 4th 1849, as part of a grand scheme to link the Great Western Railway with the Channel ports, thus avoiding London.

After coming to an agreement with the LSWR, the RGRR arranged to reach Guildford by using part of the new Guildford - Alton branch (which was under construction) at what was to become known as Ash Junction.

The section of the RGRR line from Farnborough to Ash Junction opened on August 20th 1849, coinciding with the opening of the first section of the Guildford - Alton branch from Guildford to Ash Junction. On October 8th 1849, the Alton branch was opened as far as Farnham, and finally from Farnham to Alton on July 28th 1852. The same year, the RGRR became part of the South Eastern Railway, who had operated the line since it opened.

The Guildford - Alton branch played a large part in the transformation of Aldershot from a small remote hamlet in 1855 (consisting of a church, two important houses called Aldershot Manor and Aldershot Place, two or three farmhouses and a village green), into the most important military town in the country. At first, Ash Green Station was used for handling the building materials, but later when sidings were added to the station at Tongham, which was nearer, the work was switched.

The contractor responsible for building much of the new camp at Aldershot, including the Royal Pavilion, was George Myers who, on March 15th 1855 agreed terms with the LSWR to build a temporary line from Tongham to Aldershot, in order to speed up the construction work. The route for this contractors line went from a trailing junction facing north-east at a point between Tongham and Ash Green stations, near Bin Wood, and turned north-west towards Aldershot, running between the present day site of the Greyhound Inn and the former site of the Bricklayers Arms at Ash. From here the line crossed North Lane, south of Thorn Hill, and then ran parallel with the High Street finishing just short of the Farnborough Road, now the A325. When building was considered to be completed, the contractors line was removed.

As Aldershot continued to grow, the local inhabitants felt that they needed their own station and, after coming up with various schemes of their own, they managed to persuade the LSWR to build a line from a junction near Pirbright, on the main London - Basingstoke line, to join the Guildford - Alton line between Tongham and Farnham at what became known as Farnham Junction. This new line opened on May 2nd 1870 and provided a station, not only at Aldershot, but also at Ash Vale (originally named North Camp & Ash Vale, not to be confused with the present day North Camp Station, which was also in use at the time), while the section of track between Farnham Junction and Farnham was doubled at the same time, although from Farnham to Alton remained single until June 2nd 1901.

By this time, the original line to Alton had been extended in 1865 by the Mid-Hants Railway (originally known as the Alton, Alresford and Winchester Railway) for 17 miles, to a junction on the main London-Southampton line, just 2 miles north of Winchester.

During this period, the *Surrey Advertiser* reported a very sad occasion in their Tuesday May 16th 1865 edition as follows:-

Tongham

Sudden Death - On Thursday morning, John Wiseman, porter at the Tongham Station of the South Western Railway, was attacked by a malady and ended his life in a few hours. He complained that something was the matter with his throat, and a surgeon was called in, who prescribed for him, but pronounced the case a bad one. Mrs. Wiseman shortly afterwards started to fetch some medicine from Farnham, and on her return she found that her husband was dead. The deceased has left a family of young children; but we are glad to hear that he belonged to the Manchester Unity of Odd Fellows, and was a subscriber to the Widows and Orphans Fund.

There was more drama at Ash Green Station on August 27th 1874, when a horse box and carriage were detached from a Guildford to Southampton train, while a wagon containing the furniture of a signalman who was being transferred, was attached. The train reversed to regain the detached horse box and carriage but, unfortunately experienced coupling trouble which resulted in the two vehicles running back down the 1 in 121 gradient towards Ash Junction. As the guard tried scotching the wheels, four passengers jumped clear while a porter threw ballast on the rails. The two vehicles gained speed and headed towards the junction, where they unfortunately collided with a passing South Eastern Railway goods train.

A train approaching Tongham Station from Guildford in 1897.   M.C.Lawson Collection

5

With the new, more direct line from Pirbright Junction via Aldershot to Farnham opening in 1870, the original line from Ash Junction to Farnham Junction became known as the Tongham loop and, in many ways, it was the beginning of the end for this section, which started to lose some of its importance. The situation was not helped by a further development which took place in 1879, when a spur was opened to link the South Eastern Railway station at Ash with Aldershot, and from then on even some of the Guildford to Farnham traffic started to use this new spur, and continued to do so, even though the line between Ash Green and Farnham Junction was doubled on June 4th 1884.

Looking south from the approach road towards the station building at Tongham, which can just be seen on the bridge (left of centre of the photograph). Ricketts the butchers, later Sturts is on the right of the photograph.   M.C.Lawson Collection

Tongham Station during the early 1900's.   M.C.Lawson Collection

Tragedy struck the Tongham loop when Mr. Jim Burt, the signalman at Tongham Station, was accidentally killed on October 19th 1885, when he was crushed between two wagons while shunting was taking place.

On September 1st 1891, the last station in the area was opened at Wanborough, between Guildford and Ash Junction, at the request of Sir Algernon West, the personal Private Secretary of the then Prime Minister, Mr. Gladstone. Sir Algernon lived at Wanborough Manor and was also a director of the LSWR.

In 1856, a Gas Works was opened at Aldershot, on the north side of Ash Road, near the Blackwater River. Coal was received via Tongham Station, from where it was carted by horse to the works.

A direct line from Tongham Station to the Gas Works was first suggested in October 1889, but it was not until the Aldershot Gas & Water Act of 1896, that permission was granted.

Tenders were received for the construction of this new line, which would be about ³/₄ mile in length and run north from a trailing connection just west of Tongham Station. The contract was awarded in May 1898 to Thomas Turner of Blackwater, while the contract for the steel incline and bridge over Ash Road was awarded to Sir William Arrol & Co.

The line to the Gas Works was opened for business by October 1898, and because LSWR locomotives were not permitted to use this line, the Gas Works Company purchased their own locomotive from W.G.Bagnall Ltd. of Stafford, a 0-4-0 saddle tank which had originally been obtained by W.G.Bagnall from Henry Hughes & Company of Loughborough. The locomotive was later christened "Patricia" after the elder daughter of Mr.R.W.Edwards, Chairman of what was then called the Aldershot Gas, Water & District Lighting Company.

An aerial view of Aldershot Gas Works in 1927.   Author's Collection

7

In 1923, the LSWR became part of the newly formed Southern Railway, who later decided to make the following changes: firstly, on December 1st 1926, both Ash Green and Tongham stations were reduced to unstaffed halts and Ash Green was also closed to goods; then the double lines from Ash Junction to Farnham Junction were singled on February 9th 1930; finally the sparse passenger service was discontinued on July 4th 1937, although the line stayed open for goods to Tongham and to serve the Gas Works.

On August 22nd 1940, an ammunition train made up of 47 wagons was standing on the single line between Tongham and Farnham Junction when a bomb hit one of 6 open wagons, exploding the contents and sending shells all over the railway. Two of the Southern Railway employees who lived nearby, ganger George Keen and lengthman George Leach, were awarded the George Medal for their courage after they had separated the burning wagons from the rest of the train.

After nationalization in 1948, the Southern Railway passed into the hands of British Railways Southern Region. As by the early 1950's the goods service was down to two trains per day, the new owners decided that from November 21st 1954,

the rarely used section of track between Farnham Junction and Tongham should be taken out of use, making Ash Junction the only means of access to the line.

By 1960, when the goods service was down to two trains per week and the service to the Gas Works had ceased, it was decided to close the line completely from December 31st 1960.

A poor quality view of a passenger waiting on the 'down' platform at Ash Green in 1900. Author's Collection

Ash Green Station in 1900, looking towards Ash Junction. It is understood, that Queen Victoria used this station when she first reviewed her troops at Aldershot. M.C.Lawson Collection

An early postcard view of Tongham Station, looking towards Ash Green.

The Tongham yard gang c.1920. (*Left to right*) Mr.Barnes, Mr.Percy (ganger), Mr.Forder, Mr.Rodgers (sub-ganger) and Mr.Freeman.

Description of the Route

Ash Junction to Farnham Junction

On leaving Ash Junction, the line soon passed under the Drovers Way girder bridge and climbed at 1 in 121 for about 60 chains to reach Ash Green Station which, as mentioned in the history of the line, was a very active place when first opened, by handling all the original building materials for the new military camp at Aldershot. This work was later switched to Tongham Station after sidings were added and a temporary contractors line was built from Tongham to Aldershot to speed up the construction work.

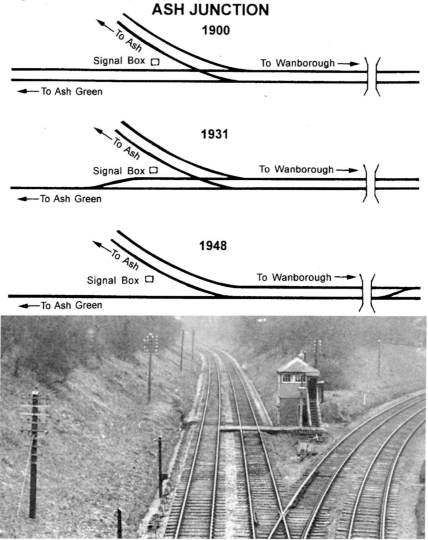

ASH JUNCTION

1900

To Ash

Signal Box ▢

To Ash Green ◀—

To Wanborough ➡

1931

To Ash

Signal Box ▢

To Ash Green ◀—

To Wanborough ➡

1948

To Ash

Signal Box ▢

To Ash Green ◀—

To Wanborough ➡

An early view of Ash Junction showing double tracks leading straight ahead towards Tongham.

Author's Collection

10

After the Tongham line was singled in1930 but before it was further altered in 1936. M.C.Lawson Collection

Maunsell N class 2-6-0 No.31867 on the 12.05 p.m. Reading to Redhill train, passing the now completely single track to Tongham at Ash Junction on January 19th 1952. Denis Cullum

Bulleid Q1 class 0-6-0 No.33019 on the single track approaching Ash Junction on December 24th 1960.
D.Lawrence

ASH GREEN STATION

1900

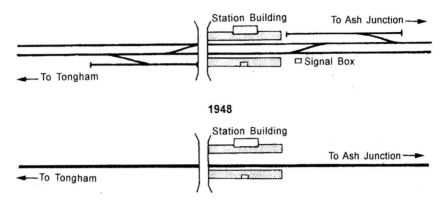

1948

The station building was at street level, with a covered corrugated staircase leading down to the 'up' platform. After the line was doubled in 1884, the layout consisted of 'up' and 'down' platforms with sidings on both sides of the lines, plus a signal box on the 'down' side. On May 17th 1927 the sidings and signal box were taken out of use, and when the line was singled on February 9th 1930, the 'up' line was removed, which meant that passengers not only had to come down the covered staircase to the disused platform, but also had to cross over the track to the original 'down' platform, which now served both directions. At least there was a small wooden shelter on this platform for the few passengers who used this station.

The former station (later Halt) at Ash Green in 1960 looking towards Ash Junction with the Drovers Way bridge in the distance.

Lens of Sutton

A street level view of the former station building at Ash Green. The covered corrugated staircase leading down to the platforms can be seen on the left of the photograph. Author's Collection

The former station at Ash Green during the same period, looking towards Tongham. The bottom part of the covered corrugated staircase from street level is on the right side of the building. Lens of Sutton

After passing under the White Lane brick bridge, the line continued from Ash Green, partly in a cutting, by first gently dropping at 1 in 1295 followed by 1 in 206 and passed under a footbridge, before approaching Tongham on a very slight climb of 1 in 930, 1 mile 74 chains from Ash Junction.

Tongham Station was in some ways similar to Ash Green, in that the station building was at street level, with a covered staircase down to the 'up' platform but, unlike Ash Green, Tongham booking hall was facing the road on the west side of the brick road bridge, which crossed the line.

This view looking towards the goods yard at Tongham Station, was taken from the footbridge on the approach to the station from Ash Green. Author's Collection

The station building at Tongham in the early 1900's. The booking hall was facing the road on the west side of the brick bridge which crossed the line. Lens of Sutton

The layout consisted of several sidings east of the station off the 'up' line, and a signal box on the 'down' side, whilst west of the station, the line to the Gas Works trailed off north-west through a gate from the 'up' line, and a short siding through a gate into Hyde's dog biscuit factory ran off the 'down' line in an easterly direction behind the platform. After the line was singled on February 9th 1930, passengers only used the 'down' platform, although the section of track on the 'up' side of the station remained as a loop for connections to the Gas Works, and also the sidings on the east side of the station. The signal box closed at the same time as the line was singled and from then on, all the sidings were worked from ground frames. Hyde's siding was also out of use at this period but was brought back into use as McCarthy's siding on May 23rd 1944. A War Office siding was also added south of the line on the east side of the station sometime during the early 1940's.

TONGHAM STATION

1897

To Gas Works

Gate

Station Building

Loading Dock

To Ash Green →

←To Farnham
Junction

Gate

□ Signal Box

1955

To Gas Works

Gate

Station Building

Loading Dock

To Ash Green →

Gate

War Office Siding

Tongham Station, looking towards Ash Green on September 26th 1953.   S.C.Nash

15

Activity at Tongham Station in the early part of the 1900's.

Tongham Station in 1916. The poster on the left mentions blackouts to prevent air raids from Zeppelins. The poster on right (above the horse) asks schoolboys to help with the harvest.

(*Left*) Arthur Binsted the Tongham Stationmaster in the 1930's. Note how the lettering on the nameboard is white with a black background compared to the two earlier photographs on the opposite page. Ann Hollaway Collection (*Right*) A group of people standing on the track and loading dock at Tongham on September 28th 1953 while the Railway Enthusiasts' Club special "Hants & Surrey Tour" train waits at the down platform in the station. Author's Collection

Bulleid Q1 class 0-6-0 No.33019 with a brake van under the bridge at Tongham Station on December 29th 1960. In the mid 1950's, the main street level station building was demolished and a metal footbridge was built next to the bridge on the west side from which, at the time, the covered staircase still existed.
H.Davies

From Tongham, the line continued on the level and passed under two brick bridges, first the St.Georges Road bridge followed by a bridge which carried a small lane leading to Badshot Farm before reaching Farnham Junction, 3 miles 70 chains from Ash Junction.

The down platform at Tongham Station looking towards Farnham Junction.

Lens of Sutton

Marker light at the approach to Tongham from Farnham Junction on September 26th 1953. S.C.Nash

FARNHAM JUNCTION

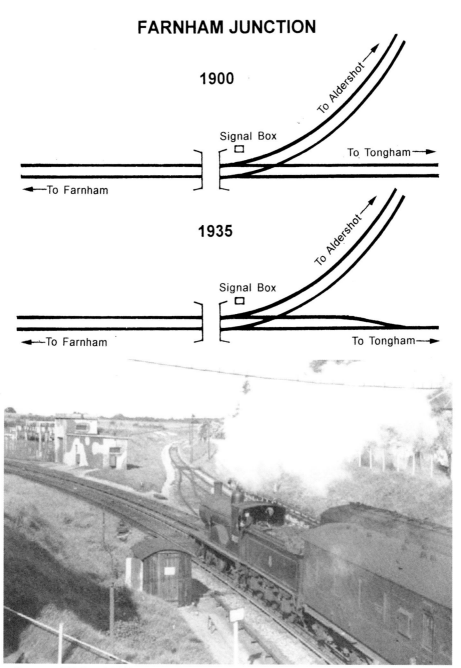

1900

To Aldershot →

Signal Box

To Tongham →

← To Farnham

1935

To Aldershot →

Signal Box

← To Farnham

To Tongham →

Drummond T9 class 4-4-0 No.30307 pulls an up parcels train towards Aldershot from Farnham, passing the Tongham line (centre of photograph) at Farnham Junction.   E.C.Griffiths

The signal box at Farnham Junction.

Drummond L12 class 4-4-0 No.30434 pulls the Railway Enthusiasts' Club special "Hants & Surrey Tour" train to Bordon past the Tongham line at Farnham Junction on September 26th 1953.

Motive Power and Rolling Stock

When the line first opened to Farnham, and later Alton, there is no doubt that many early interesting examples of LSWR locomotives and rolling stock could be seen - operating from Guildford. By the 1860's and 70's, the Joseph Beattie 'Nelson' and 'Saxon' class 2-4-0 locomotives worked the line, followed by his Double and Single Framed Goods 0-6-0's. Later, the passenger service was mainly handled by Adams locomotives, ranging from his 0415 'Radial' class 4-4-2T's to his A12 'Jubilee' class 0-4-2's and 0395 'Jumbo' class 0-6-0's. Various Drummond locomotives, including his M7 class 0-4-4T's, were also in use, and his 700 class 0-6-0 tender engines helped to handle the goods traffic after the passenger service was discontinued on July 4th 1937.

By the late 1940's, the goods traffic was in the hands of Maunsell U class 2-6-0's and finally Bulleid Q1 class 0-6-0's.

Although the early coaching stock is unclear, the sparse passenger service was later handled with short two coach sets consisting of six-wheel and later bogie stock, while pull-and-push two coach sets were also used.

In the early 1900's, Drummond H13 class Steam Railcars saw service between Guildford and Farnham, although these mainly worked via Aldershot.

As previously mentioned, the Gas Works obtained their own locomotive, a 0-4-0 saddle tank, from W.G.Bagnall Ltd. of Stafford, which was originally built by Henry Hughes & Co. of Loughborough, and was later called "Patricia". Other locomotives owned by the Gas Works at various times were two Aveling & Porter 0-4-0's, called "Louisa" and "Kathleen", and finally two Peckett 0-4-0 saddle tanks.

Maunsell U class 2-6-0 No.1621 with coal for Aldershot Gas Works, entering the Tongham line at Ash Junction.

E.C.Griffiths

Adams 0415 'Radial' class 4-4-2T No.169 at Farnham Station in 1900. M.C.Lawson Collection

The 0-4-0 saddle tank "Patricia", owned by the Aldershot Gas Works. M.C.Lawson Collection

Bulleid Q1 class 0-6-0 No.33019 at Ash Junction on December 24th 1960. D.Lawrence

Operation

When the line originally opened, signal boxes were required at Ash Junction, Ash Green, Tongham and Farnham. Later, when the line was extended from Farnham to Alton, boxes were added at both Bentley and Alton.

After the line from Aldershot joined the Tongham-Farnham section, a box was added at Farnham Junction. On May 17th 1927, the sidings at Ash Green were taken out of use and the signal box was closed. On February 9th 1930, when the whole section of line from Farnham Junction to Ash Junction was reduced to a single track, the signal box at Tongham was also closed and the sidings were worked from ground frames.

Southern Railway Sectional Appendix. March 26th 1934.

TONGHAM.

The up siding terminates with buffer stops about 327 yards the Farnham Junction side and about 537 yards the Ash Junction side of Tongham station respectively.

Connections between the single line and the siding are provided at both ends of the siding, and are operated from ground frames controlled by the key-token for the Farnham Junction and Ash Junction section.

An intermediate key-token instrument is provided to enable a train to be shunted clear of the running line and after this has been done, to restore to normal the key-token working between Ash Junction and Farnham Junction, and so enable trains to pass through the section in either direction under ordinary key-token working. In connection with this arrangement, the provisions of Regulation 34 A, of the Electric Train Tablet or Staff Regulations must be observed.

On the arrival of a train at the siding the key must be inserted in the lock of the point lever and the points set for the siding, and when the train has entered the siding, clear of the main line, the points must be re-set for the main line.

The key-token must then be taken out of the lock on the point lever and inserted in the intermediate instrument and the Signalmen at Ash Junction and Farnham Junction advised by telephone that the running line is clear.

When the train requires to leave the siding after the use of the intermediate instrument as before described, permission must first be obtained by telephone from the Signalmen at Ash Junction and Farnham Junction, and the Signalmen must be informed in which direction the train is about to travel. The Signalmen, provided the key-token instruments are in their normal position and the line is clear in accordance with Block Regulation 4, will give what instructions are necessary affecting the journey from the siding to the signal box concerned; the key-token in the intermediate instrument must then be given one quarter turn towards the " out " position and the Signalmen advised that everything is in readiness for the key-token to be withdrawn. The Signalmen must thereupon depress and hold in their respective bell plungers, which action will place the siding galvanometer needle to " free " and thus allow the key-token to be completely turned to the " out " position and withdrawn. An indication that the key-token has been withdrawn from the intermediate instrument will be given by a movement of the galvanometer needles in Ash Junction and Farnham Junction boxes.

After the key-token has been withdrawn from the intermediate instrument the Signalmen at Ash Junction and Farnham Junction must be so advised by telephone, and the usual working in accordance with the instructions shown in clauses (a) and (b) of Regulation 34 of the Electric Train Tablet or Staff Regulations will be resumed.

Gradient Profile

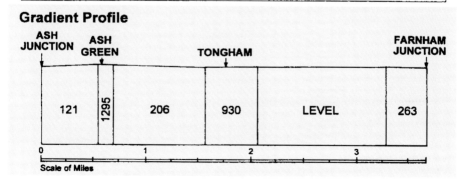

ASH JUNCTION	ASH GREEN		TONGHAM		FARNHAM JUNCTION
121	1295	206	930	LEVEL	263

Scale of Miles

23

Timetables and Tickets

APRIL 1910

GUILDFORD and FARNHAM.—London and South Western.

Down.		Week Days.		Sundays.
	mrn mrn mrn mrn	aft aft aft	aft aft	mrn mrn aft
Mls Guildford....dep.	6 40 7 10 10 30 12 28	2 53 4 8 5 53	6 50 8 13	8 13 10 18 6 50
4½ Wanborough	6 40 8 3 11 0 12 42	2 15 3 56 0 8	7 0 8 23	8 23 10 28 7 0
6 Ash Green	6 56 8 9 11 8 12 49	2 21 4 3 6 14	7 8 8 31	8 31 10 36 7 8
7½ Tongham	7 0 8 13 11 10 12 53	2 25 4 6 6 18	7 10 8 35	8 35 10 40 7 10
10½ Farnham 137 arr	7 8 8 20 11 16 12 59	2 32 4 13 6 24	7 17 8 41	8 41 10 46 7 18

Up.		Week Days.		Sundays.
	mrn mrn mrn	aft aft aft	aft aft aft aft aft	mrn aft
Farnham ......dep.	8 0 9 13 11 11	2 4 4 22 5 28 7 36 8 40 9 43	9 5 9 18
Tongham	8 7 9 21 11 8	2 12 4 29 6 5 7 34 8 48 9 50	9 12 9 25
Ash Green	8 11 9 25 11 22	2 16 4 33 6 8 7 33 8 52 9 54	9 16 9 29
Wanborough 194, 349	8 16 9 30 11 27	2 21 4 39 6 14 7 43 8 57 9 59	9 21 9 34
Guildford 155, 166	8 24 9 39 11 35	2 29 4 46 6 25 7 51 9 6 10 7	9 29 9 42

m Motor Car, 1st and 3rd class.

JULY 1922

GUILDFORD and FARNHAM.—London and South Western.

Miles	Down.		Week Days only.	
		mrn mrn mrn	e mrn mrn aft aft aft aft aft aft	aft
	152 London (W. 156 dep	5 50 6 50	7 0 9 11 7 12 50 2 7 3 50 5 0 6 10 7	
	Guildford ....dep	6 50 8 0	8 40 10 6 11 51 4 9 3 24 4 0 6 47 8 8 23	
4½	Wanborough	8 8 8 49	10 14 12 3 1 50 3 4 4 49 6 127 16 8 31	
6	Ash Green S	8 13 8 53	10 19 12 8 1 55 3 48 4 53 6 17 7 21 8 38	
7½	Tongham	8 17 8 57	10 23 12 12 1 59 3 52 4 57 6 21 7 23 8 40	
10½	Farnham 126, 130 arr	7 0 8 24 9 0	10 29 12 18 2 5 3 58 5 0 6 27 7 31 8 40	

Miles	Up.		Week Days only.	
		mrn mrn	mrn aft aft aft aft aft aft aft	aft
	Farnham ......dep	8 0 9 0	10 52 1 0 2 23 4 23 5 20 6 35 7 45 8 51	
3	Tongham	8 7 9 7	10 59 1 7 2 35 4 30 5 27 6 42 7 53 8 58	
4½	Ash Green S	8 11 9 11	11 3 1 11 2 39 4 34 5 31 6 46 7 57 9 2	
6	Wanborough	8 16 9 16	11 8 1 16 2 44 4 39 5 36 6 51 8 2 9 7	
10½	Guildford 154, 157 arr	8 24 9 24	11 16 1 24 2 52 4 47 5 44 6 59 8 10 9 15	
40½	154 London W. 157 arr	9 12 10 11	12 6 3 0 4 6 5 50 7 0 7 56 8 10 10 45	

c Runs to Alton, see page 126.   S About ½ mile to Ash Station (S. E. & C.).

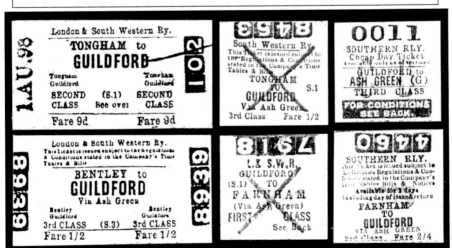

London & South Western Ry.
TONGHAM to **GUILDFORD**
Tongham / Guildford — Tongham / Guildford
SECOND CLASS (S.1) See over — SECOND CLASS
Fare 9d / Fare 9d — 1 AU 98 — 102

8978 South Western Ry. This Ticket is issued subject to the Regulations & Conditions stated in the Company's Time Tables &c. **TONGHAM** TO **GUILDFORD** Via Ash Green — S.1 — 3rd Class Fare 1/2

0011 SOUTHERN RLY. Cheap Day Ticket Available only as advertised **GUILDFORD** to **ASH GREEN (G)** THIRD CLASS FOR CONDITIONS SEE BACK

London & South Western Ry. This Ticket is issued subject to the regulations & Conditions stated in the Company's Time Tables & Bills **BENTLEY** to **GUILDFORD** Via Ash Green Bentley / Guildford — Bentley / Guildford 3rd CLASS (S.3) 3rd CLASS Fare 1/2 / Fare 1/2 — 8938

8154 L & S.W.R. **GUILDFORD** (S.1) TO **FARNHAM** (Via Ash Green) FIRST CLASS See Back

0977 SOUTHERN RLY. This Ticket is issued subject to the regulations & Conditions stated in the Company's Time Tables Bills & Notices Available for 3 days including day of issue & return **FARNHAM** TO **GUILDFORD** VIA ASH GREEN 3rd Class. Fare 2/4

Tickets from the G.R.Croughton Collection

Special Visits

Like many similar lines which had either recently closed or were still open for goods only, the Tongham line received some interesting special trains.

On September 26th 1953, the Railway Enthusiasts' Club of Farnborough special train called "Hants & Surrey Tour", pulled by Drummond L12 class 4-4-0 No. 30434, visited the line on a trip from North Camp Station to Ash Green and Tongham via Guildford. Although it was hoped to continue from Tongham through to Farnham Junction, this section of line was considered to be unsuitable, so, the train returned to Guildford, before embarking on a non-stop run to Kingsley Halt and then Bordon.

The Railway Enthusiasts' Club ran another special to Ash Green and Tongham on October 5th 1957, which was called "The Compass Rose" and was pulled by Drummond M7 class 0-4-4T No. 30051 and covered goods only lines and little used spurs in Hampshire, Surrey and Berkshire.

Drummond L12 class 4-4-0 No.30434 pulls the Railway Enthusiasts' Club special "Hants & Surrey Tour" train past Ash Junction on its way to Guildford on September 26th 1953.   S.C.Nash

The same special train heading for Tongham at about halfway between Ash Green and Tongham on September 26th 1953.   S.C.Nash

The Railway Enthusiasts' Club special "Hants & Surrey Tour" train waits at the former down platform at Tongham Station while the engine runs round the train on September 26th 1953. The line to the Aldershot Gas Works can just be seen turning to the right at the far end of the up platform.
Author's Collection

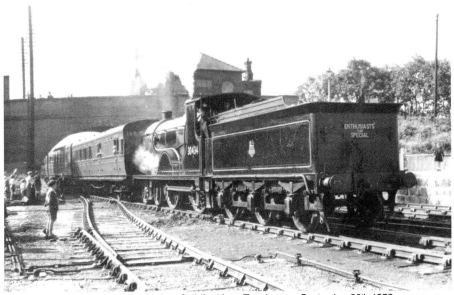

The same special train starting back to Guildford from Tongham on September 26th 1953.   S.C.Nash

The Railway Enthusiasts' Club special train "The Compass Rose" with Drummond M7 class 0-4-4T No.30051 and pull-and-push set No.721 at Ash Green on October 5th 1957. R.N.Thornton

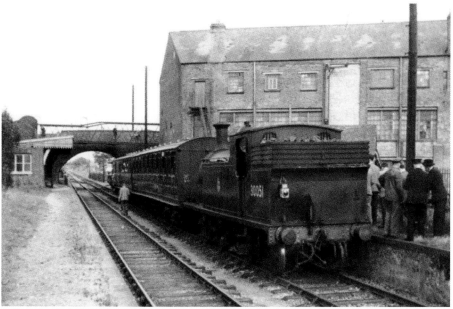

The same train at Tongham Station on October 5th 1957. By this time, the main street level station building had been removed to make way for a metal footbridge, next to the road bridge. The covered staircase (left of photograph) which remained, can just be seen above the platform shelter. R.M.Casserley

Final Closure

Once the coal traffic for the Gas Works ceased in the late 1950's, the twice weekly goods service to Tongham was not considered enough reason to keep the line open, so British Railways Southern Region decided that the last revenue-earning goods train to call at Tongham would be on December 31st 1960.

The final train was pulled by Bulleid Q1 class 0-6-0 No. 33025, in the hands of driver Plumpton and fireman Ansell, both of Guildford, and steamed into Tongham at 10.05 a.m., where it was met by senior porter White of Farnham. In the brake van with guard Wickens of Guildford were several members of the Railway Enthusiasts' Club of Farnborough, who had come to pay their last respects to this local line.

Driver Plumpton and fireman Ansell pose on Bulleid Q1 class 0-6-0 No.33025 while guard Wickens and senior porter White stand on the track at Tongham with the last goods train on December 31st 1960.   M.H.Walshaw

The signal box at Ash Junction stayed open until April 1st 1963, while the very overgrown track remained in position until the points were removed on April 4th 1965.

Although the section of track between Farnham Junction and Tongham had been taken out of use on November 21st 1954, the signal box at Farnham Junction remained open until May 5th 1964, and was finally demolished in 1966.

Bulleid Q1 class 0-6-0 No.33025 with the last goods train at Tongham on December 31st 1960.
H.Davies

Looking at the brake van on the last goods train at Tongham on December 31st 1960.   H.Davies

The Present Scene

The site of Ash Junction is now completely overgrown with trees and is impossible to spot when looking from the existing line between Wanborough and Ash stations, (compare with pages 10 and 11) although, beyond the trees the trackbed now forms a footpath from the former junction via Ash Green towards Tongham.

The station building at Ash Green is now a private residence with what appears to be the covered staircase and former 'up' platform still in tact, but fenced off from the public. The very overgrown 'down' platform is also still visible.

From the former station at Ash Green, the footpath continues towards Tongham but, on approaching Tongham, the line comes to an abrupt end at the site of the footbridge where a housing development has been built on the former route.

' Although the station building at Tongham was demolished in the mid 1950's, the road bridge, which crossed the former track, and for many people the one remaining landmark which told them that a railway once went through the village at this spot, was removed in 1994 and now giving no evidence that a railway was ever there.

Much of the former route between Tongham and Farnham Junction, plus the line to the Gas Works, has completely disappeared under the road development which now links the A31 Hogs Back road and the M3 motorway.

The site of Farnham Junction (near the A31 road bridge), is now also like the site of Ash Junction and is very overgrown and impossible to spot from the existing line between Aldershot and Farnham stations.

The site of Ash Junction and signal box (centre of the photograph) on November 19th 2018. See pages 10 and 11 to compare this view.   Author

(*Left*) The road bridge at Tongham, just before it was demolished in January 1994. M.C.Lawson (*Right*) The former trackbed which is now a footpath looking towards Ash Green on the approach from Tongham on December 3rd 2018. Author

(*Left*) The remains of the former down platform at Ash Green under the road bridge on December 3rd 2018. Author (*Right*) The former station house at Ash Green on the same day. Author

The site of Farnham Junction to the right of the electrical substation (on the right side of the photograph) on November 19th 2018. See pages 19 and 20 to compare this view. Author

Conclusion

After the original line from Guildford to Alton was opened, the stations at Ash Green and Tongham seemed to have a rosy future, but once Aldershot developed and received its own station in 1870 on a new line from Pirbright Junction, and later when the spur was opened from Ash to Aldershot in 1875, the future of the sections from Ash Junction to Farnham Junction would appear to be doomed.

The opening of a short branch from Tongham to Aldershot Gas Works in 1898 was no doubt the main reason why the line stayed open for so long, even though the sparse passenger service was discontinued in 1937.

Once the coal for the Gas Works was discontinued and the goods service to Tongham was down to two days a week, the line finally closed in 1960.

Acknowledgements

Many thanks to all the people who kindly helped by providing information and photographs for the original printing of this publication in 1994, particularly the late Maurice Lawson who had been interested in the Tongham railway for many years and carried out much research on the line. Unfortunately, like Maurice Lawson, many of the other people who helped with the original edition have sadly passed on but, I would still like to put on record my thanks to everyone and especially to all the photographers whose names are listed under the photographs.

For this printing, I would like to thank Norman Branch for reading my text and to James Christian of Binfield Print & Design Limited for his help.

Bibliography

The LSWR Volume 1 & 2 by R.A.Williams (*David & Charles*)
WOKING TO ALTON by Vic Mitchell & Keith Smith (*Middleton Press*)
THE RAILWAYS OF SOUTHERN ENGLAND: SECONDARY AND BRANCH LINES
by Edwin Course (*Batsford*)
RAILWAY MAGAZINES (*Various issues*)

The road bridge and steel footbridge at the former Tongham Station looking towards Ash Green in July 1975 before both brick bridge and steel bridge were later removed in 1994.   Nick Catford